Stories
of
GREAT PEOPLE

Julius Caesar's sandals

Gerry Bailey and Karen Foster
Illustrated by Leighton Noyes
and Q2M

WITHDRAWN

🍄 Crabtree Publishing Company
www.crabtreebooks.com

DIGBY PLATT is an antique collector. Every Saturday he picks up a bargain at Mr. Rummage's antique stall and loves listening to the story behind his new 'find'.

Mr. RUMMAGE has a stall piled high with interesting objects—and he has a great story to tell about each and every one of his treasures.

COLONEL KARBUNCLE sells military uniforms, medals, flags, swords, helmets, cannon balls—all from the trunk of his old jeep.

HANNAH PLATT is Digby's argumentative, older sister—and she doesn't believe a word that *Mr. Rummage* says!

![Crabtree Publishing Company logo]

Crabtree Publishing Company
www.crabtreebooks.com

Other books in the series

Armstrong's moon rock

Cleopatra's coin

Columbus's chart

Galileo's telescope

Leonardo's palette

Marco Polo's silk purse

Martin Luther King Jr.'s microphone

Mother Teresa's alms bowl

Mozart's wig

Queen Victoria's diamond

Shakespeare's quill

Sitting Bull's tomahawk

The Wright Brothers' glider

Credits

AKG Images: p. 16 (top right); Peter Connolly: p. 25 (center left), 29 (top right); Palazzo Madama, Rome: p. 21 (bottom left); Pinacoteca Nazionale, Siena/ Rabatti – Domingie: p. 31 (top right)

Prisma/Ancient Art & Architecture Collection: p. 23 (bottom left)

Art Archive: Bibliothèque des Arts Décoratifs Paris / Dagli Orti: p. 11 (top); Museo Civico Trieste / Dagli Orti: p. 13 (top right); Museo della Civilta Romana Rome / Dagli Orti: p. 11 (bottom); Palazzo Pitti Florence / Dagli Orti: p. 9 (center right)

Bridgeman Art Library: Museo Archeologico Nazionale, Naples: p. 16 (bottom left); Museo e Gallerie Nazionali di Capodimonte, Naples, Italy: p. 35 (center right); National Gallery of Scotland, Edinburgh: p. 31 (center left); V & A Museum, London: p. 20 (top right)

iStockphoto.com: p. 20 (center left)

Mary Evans Picture Library: p. 25 (bottom right), 26 (top right), 27, 29 (bottom left), 33 (top right)

Ann Ronan PL/HIP/Topfoto: p. 23 (top right)

Werner Forman Archive: p. 15 (bottom)

Picture research: Diana Morris. info@picture-research.co.uk
Editor: Lynn Peppas
Proofreaders: David Hurd, Crystal Sikkens
Project editor: Robert Walker
Prepress technician: Ken Wright
Production coordinator: Margaret Amy Salter

Library and Archives Canada Cataloguing in Publication

Bailey, Gerry
  Julius Caesar's sandals / Gerry Bailey and Karen Foster ; illustrated by Leighton Noyes and Q2M.

(Stories of great people)
Includes index.
ISBN 978-0-7787-3695-0 (bound).--ISBN 978-0-7787-3717-9 (pbk.)

  1. Caesar, Julius--Juvenile fiction. 2. Heads of state--Rome-- Biography--Juvenile fiction. 3. Generals--Rome--Biography--Juvenile fiction. 4. Rome--History--Republic, 265-30 B.C.--Juvenile fiction. 5. Caesar, Julius--Juvenile literature. 6. Heads of state--Rome-- Biography--Juvenile literature. 7. Generals--Rome--Biography--Juvenile literature. 8. Rome--History--Republic, 265-30 B.C.--Juvenile literature. I. Foster, Karen, 1959- II. Noyes, Leighton III. Q2M (Firm) IV. Title. V. Series.

PZ7.B15Ju 2008   j823'.92   C2008-907028-3

Library of Congress Cataloging-in-Publication Data

Bailey, Gerry.
  Julius Caesar's sandals / Gerry Bailey and Karen Foster ; illustrated by Leighton Noyes and Q2M.
       p. cm. -- (Stories of great people)
  Includes index.
  ISBN 978-0-7787-3717-9 (pbk. : alk. paper) -- ISBN 978-0-7787-3695-0 (reinforced library binding : alk. paper)
  1. Caesar, Julius--Juvenile literature. 2. Heads of state--Rome--Biography--Juvenile literature. 3. Generals--Rome--Biography--Juvenile literature. 4. Rome--History--Republic, 265-30 B.C.--Juvenile literature. I. Foster, Karen. II. Title. III. Series.

  DG261.B25 2009
  937'.02092--dc22
  [B]
                                                    2008046280

Crabtree Publishing Company
www.crabtreebooks.com   1-800-387-7650

Published in Canada
Crabtree Publishing
616 Welland Ave.
St. Catharines, Ontario
L2M 5V6

Published in the United States
Crabtree Publishing
PMB16A
350 Fifth Ave., Suite 3308
New York, NY 10118

Published by CRABTREE PUBLISHING COMPANY
Copyright © **2009** Diverta Ltd.

Julius Caesar's sandals

Table of Contents

Knicknack Market comes to life	6
Julius Caesar	9
School days	11
Ambitious youth	13
In the ring	15
Duel to the death!	16
Early Rome	20
Rise to power	21
Governor of Gaul	23
Barbarian tribes	25
Romans and Celts	26
The Rubicon	29
Up the Nile	31
Power at last!	33
Assassinated!	35
Historical notes	36
Glossary and Index	37

Every Saturday morning, Knicknack Market comes to life. The street vendors are there almost before the sun is up. And by the time you and I are out of bed, the stalls are built, the boxes are opened, and all the goods are carefully laid out on display.

Objects are piled high. Some are laid out on velvet: precious necklaces and jeweled swords. Others stand upright at the back:

large, framed pictures of very important people, lamps made from tasseled satin, and old-fashioned cash registers—the kind that jingle when the drawers are opened. And then there are things that stay in their boxes all day, waiting for the right

customer to come along: war medals laid out in straight lines, stopwatches on leather straps, and utensils in polished silver for all those special occasions.

But Mr. Rummage's stall is different. Mr. Rummage of Knicknack Market has a stall piled high with a disorderly jumble of things that no one could ever want. Who'd want to buy a stuffed mouse? Or a broken umbrella? Or a pair of false teeth?

Well, Mr. Rummage has them all. And, as you can imagine, they don't cost a lot!

Digby Platt—ten year-old collector of antiques—was off to see his friend Mr. Rummage of Knicknack Market. It was Saturday and, as usual, Digby's weekly allowance was burning a hole in his pocket.

But Digby wasn't going to spend it on any old thing. It had to be something rare and interesting for his collection, something from Mr. Rummage's incredible stall. Hannah, his older sister, had come along too. She had secret doubts about the value of Mr. Rummage's objects and felt, for some big-sisterly reason, that she had to stop her little brother from buying useless pieces of junk.

As Hannah and Digby approached Mr. Rummage's stall, they saw a bright green jeep swing past and park alongside. It was Colonel Karbuncle's jeep. He was a retired military officer who had more war stories than Mr. Rummage!

"Hello young Digby and Hannah," said Colonel Karbuncle cheerily, as he jumped down from the driver's seat.

"Have you got anything new to sell, Colonel Karbuncle?" asked Digby, peering into the back window of the jeep.

"I have, my boy, I have," said Colonel Karbuncle. "Matter of fact, I've just got back from Italy—wonderful place, full of history and the like. Here, look at these."

"Ugh! They're just a pair of dirty old sandals," said Hannah with a grimace.

"Don't be put off by the state of them," said the Colonel. "They're quite old—over 2,000 years actually—and worn by none other than the great Julius Caesar!"

"Can I try them on?" asked Digby, as his sister wrinkled her nose.

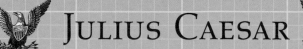

JULIUS CAESAR

Julius Caesar was born on July 12, 100 BC in Rome, in what is now Italy. He belonged to a noble family, although they were not wealthy. His mother, Aurelia, was related to influential politicians, while his father, Gaius Julius Caesar, became a *praetor* or **magistrate**, and was also governor of Asia Minor. He died when Julius was fifteen.

Statesman and soldier

Julius Caesar is best known for being a brilliant and powerful military leader. He was also a good statesman or politician. He made many changes to the old Roman **Republic** that lasted many years.

Let's find out more...

"While I was in Italy, I did a bit of research on my own family tree, you know," declared Colonel Karbuncle, importantly. "The Karbuncles go right back to a Roman senator called Carbunculus. His name means 'pimple faced,' which is unfortunate, although he was a general in Caesar's army, I'm told."

"That's great, Colonel, but what about Julius Caesar?" sniffed Hannah, looking down at her brother's wiggling toes in disgust. "Where did he live?"

"Caesar's family probably lived in a Roman town house called a *domus*, although they may have had a country home as well," replied the Colonel.

"So he lived in style, then," said Hannah.

"Actually Julius had quite an ordinary home, by Roman standards," said Mr. Rummage, who'd just appeared from behind his stall to see what was going on.

"Let me see. You would have entered the domus through a *vestibulum*, a long narrow entrance way. There might even have been shops on either side of it. From there you went into the *atrium*, a kind of open-roofed hallway with a fountain in the middle and colorful scenes painted on the walls. And on either side of this were small rooms called *cubicula*, used as bedrooms."

"Where was the kitchen?" asked Digby. "That's the most important room."

"Not to the Romans, it wasn't," answered Mr. Rummage. "The *culina* was usually a small, hot, dark room in a corner of the house where slaves did the cooking. The dining room, or *triclinium*, on the other hand, had three couches where people could recline in comfort to eat."

SCHOOL DAYS

Like most Roman boys of his class, Julius attended school seven days a week. Apart from reading, writing, and math, pupils had to learn how to speak well in public, so Julius studied Roman law and customs. Physical education and military training were also important as, one day, he would have been expected to do his duty as a soldier. Julius loved Greek culture and probably admired war heroes such as Alexander the Great and Achilles.

Playtime

When he came home from school, Julius probably played war games with his friends in the narrow alleyways that surrounded his home. Or he might have played marbles or popular board games such as backgammon and jacks in the family's shady courtyard.

Household gods

Young Julius grew up in a religious family, and would have worshiped household gods. Every day, he and his mother would have prayed and burned incense at a family shrine called a *Lorarium*. The *lors Familiaris* were the guardian spirits of the family, *Penates* was the family spirit of the food and drink, and *Manes* were the spirits of the family's dead ancestors. Other gods protected various parts of the house.

11

"The boy loved sports, of course," said Colonel Karbuncle. "Fencing, wrestling, and sword fighting. Julius was very competitive and didn't like anyone to get the better of him."

"That's true," said Mr. Rummage, "the pirate incident proves that."

"What?" asked Digby. "I didn't know Julius was a pirate too."

"He wasn't," began the Colonel, "he just had the bad luck to run into a bunch of them on the high seas."

"It all started when Julius accused a politician of bribery," explained Mr. Rummage. "He caused such a disturbance, he had to get out of Rome until things calmed down. So he set sail for the Greek island of Rhodes to work on his public speaking skills. The Greeks were great orators, or public speakers. But Julius never got there."

"His ship was captured by pirates off the island of Pharmacussa," said the Colonel, taking up the story. "They kept him prisoner for nearly forty days. Meanwhile, his shipmates were sent home to get some ransom money to pay for his release. When Julius learned the amount the pirates were asking for him—50 **talents**—he took offense and said he was worth much more!

In fact, he was so angry, he swore that as soon as they set him free, he'd return and crucify them all!"

"And did he?" asked Digby.

"Of course," said the Colonel. "Julius was a man of his word!"

AMBITIOUS YOUTH

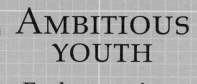

Early marriage

While he was still a boy, Julius had been engaged to a girl called Cossutia. Now that he had become interested in politics, he did not think her family was important enough for him. He broke off their agreement and married Cornelia, the daughter of a politician in the Popular party. He had become so ambitious he thought his marriage would pave the way to a powerful career.

Friends and enemies

Sulla, ruler of Rome, had his eye on Julius. He could see the young man had talent and wanted to train him. There was just one problem: Sulla was head of the Aristocratic party and he hated the Populars—so he tried to make Julius divorce Cornelia. When Julius stubbornly refused, Sulla took away Cornelia's wealth and stripped Julius of his inheritance. Julius had to go into hiding. Eventually, he was pardoned, although Sulla never trusted him again. Julius had made his first enemy.

Work experience

Julius's first real job was military assistant to Marcus Thermus, Governor General of Asia. When Thermus sent him to Bithynia to raise a fleet of ships, the young man stayed there too long. He was too busy partying, making friends with important people, and throwing his money around in courts and palaces. In the end he caused a scandal but escaped punishment because he was brave in battle. When he got back, he was given a civic crown of oak leaves!

"So Julius liked having fun," said Hannah.

"Oh yes," said the Colonel, "he was always up to something, whether it was bribing people to get himself a job, using his position to get money and power, or going down to the local arena with his friends to watch the games and bet on the players."

"Did he watch football?" asked Digby.

"Absolutely not," replied Colonel Karbuncle. "These games were blood sports where slaves called gladiators were made to fight each other, or wild animals, to entertain the crowds."

"A bit like wrestling, without rules," said Digby.

"Except that most of the time, gladiators fought to the death," said Mr. Rummage. "It was a cruel sport in cruel times."

"Sounds awful." said Hannah. "I bet the women didn't go."

"Oh yes they did," said the Colonel. "They enjoyed the blood and guts as much as the men. Some highborn women of nobel birth had favorites, or even owned gladiator slaves of their own."

"Wow!" squealed Hannah.

IN THE RING

Master of entertainment

In 65 BC Julius was made Officer in Charge of Entertainments. As well as gladiatorial games, he organized stage plays, wild beast hunts, and mock battles. Once he even filled an arena with water and staged a sea battle! He was so determined to make himself popular, that he spent vast amounts of money providing the people of Rome with enjoyable events. Sometimes, when he ran out of funds, he even persuaded his friends to pay his bills! But Julius never shared his successes. Instead, he always took the credit for himself.

Bloody arena

Roman arenas were built in the shape of a horseshoe. Stone seats were arranged in tiers—just like a modern theater—which meant you could see and hear all the action. In fact, the blood-curdling screams and curses of the dying gladiators could be heard as though you were right next to them! Julius and his guests had the best view from the royal box, where they could enjoy the show in luxury. Below, there were **arcades** for spectators to walk along, and booths where vendors sold foods such as figs, pickled hog's feet, and cakes. Here and there, shrines were built to the gods, and underground were cells for the animals and locker rooms for the gladiators.

Julius also staged chariot races at the circus. The circus was an oval-shaped racecourse with seating around the outside. People bet on their favorite teams and riders.

The charioteers would jump from the back of one horse to another as they raced. Their horses had names like *Sagitta* (Arrow) or *Rapax* (Greedy).

DUEL TO THE DEATH!

The atmosphere in the amphitheater was electric. Crowds of people flocked inside, roaring with excitement at the thought of a vicious fight that might end in bloodshed or a killing. Julius's games were so popular that many people had to sleep in tents that were pitched along the streets. And in the rush to enjoy the entertainment, the crowds often crushed people to death. Before each event, spectators entertained themselves by betting on winners—and huge sums of money changed hands.

Gladiators were mostly slaves or criminals, and were trained to fight in special schools. If they were lucky, they survived to win their freedom.

Thumbs up or thumbs down?

It was all part of the fun to dress the gladiators up in flashy armor. Julius liked to give some of the men an unfair advantage over others. So one man armed only with a small weapon and a net would be forced to defend himself against another man in full armor. When one of them was ready to make a final killing thrust, he would look up at the spectators to see if they wanted his opponent spared. If they did, they would hold up their thumbs. If not, it was thumbs down—although Julius often had the final say!

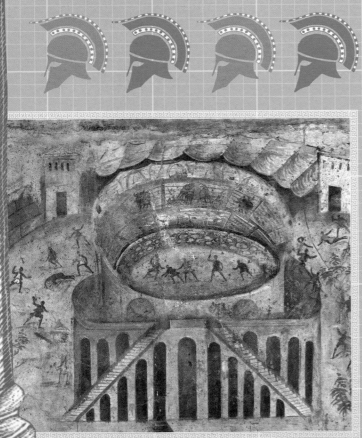

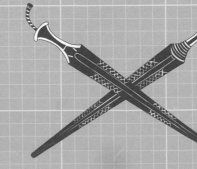

"**I**'d have been a good gladiator," said Hannah. "I'd have been the first great woman gladiator. Hannah the Great!"

"They didn't have women gladiators, silly," giggled Digby.

"That's just where you're wrong, my boy," said Colonel Karbuncle. "The Romans trained slave girls for the ring. They even had warrior stage names, like Achillia and Amazon."

"See!" smirked Hannah, spinning an imaginary sword around her head.

"I'm not sure you'd like it very much, Hannah," said Colonel Karbuncle, smiling. "If you were good, you could make a few **sesterces** on the side. You might even get to run a gladiator school of your own."

"Who wanted to be a gladiator, anyway, if it was so bad?" asked Digby.

"Most gladiators were captured enemies who had been brought back to Rome," continued the Colonel. "They were actually slaves or criminals. Being a gladiator gave them the chance of living a little longer or winning their freedom. Of course, many never lasted more than a fight or two. The lions saw to that."

"Lions! What were they doing there?" asked Hannah.

"The gladiators had to fight lions and all kinds of other wild animals," said Colonel Karbuncle. "You see why only the very good ones survived the fights?"

"But if you worked hard at gladiator school, you'd be a star?" insisted Hannah.

"Oh yes," said Colonel Karbuncle, "the really good ones became heroes and were treated very well by their owners. They made their owners lots of money from bets, so it was in the owners' interests to keep their gladiators going as long as possible."

"It sounds like Julius Caesar had loads of fun," said Digby enviously. "Rome must have been a really cool place to live."

"It was for some," said Mr. Rummage. "Not so much for the very poor or for the slaves, although some slaves were treated well. Certainly, being a slave was better than starving on the streets."

"What else can you tell us about Rome?" asked Hannah.

"Well," Mr. Rummage began, "it was a magnificent place. There was a central square called the Forum, where people could meet, listen to public speakers, and visit the market. You could buy things that came from all over the Roman **Empire**."

"Things could get a bit smelly, though," said the Colonel. "Imagine a typical Roman market on a summer's day—all sorts of meat hanging in the sweltering heat, and all the flies. Then add the sharp scent of eastern spices, musty old carpets, the smoke from fires, and the sweat of the people hurrying about their business. It would smell awful for us modern fellows."

EARLY ROME

According to legend, Rome was founded in 753 BC by the brothers Romulus and Remus. The brothers were sons of the war god Mars and were raised, it is said, by a she-wolf. They built the city on seven hills beside the River Tiber, in modern day Italy. Early Rome was ruled by kings until 509 BC. Then it became a republic ruled by **consuls** who were elected by the people. In Julius's day, Rome was the greatest power in the Mediterranean.

Model of the city of Rome which shows the Coliseum amphitheater and the Circus Maximus.

The Forum

The Roman Forum was at the heart of the ancient city and was the center of daily life. It was the main market place, a business center, and the place where religious festivals were celebrated. It was also the place you went to hear orators, or public speakers. The Romans loved talking—and Julius was no exception.

The Campus and baths

Julius often visited the Roman Campus, a track and field playground where athletes and ordinary citizens could go and exercise. People participated in foot races, jumping, wrestling, and boxing. After a hot workout, Julius would go to the public baths for a long soak, and to meet friends, chat, and relax.

Promotion for Julius

Julius had been so successful as Master of Entertainments that he was made governor of Rome's Spanish territories. On arrival in Cadiz, he admired the statue of his Greek hero, Alexander the Great. There, it is said, he sighed impatiently and remarked that, at his age, Alexander had captured most of the known world, while he, Julius, had not managed to do anything memorable yet. Spurred on to make a name for himself, he won some incredible military victories for Rome. When he got home, everyone was impressed.

RISE TO POWER

The Republic of Rome was ruled by a group of elected senators who formed the Senate, the place of government. Senator Julius was so ambitious, many other senators were afraid of him. When he tried to put on a massive gladiatorial show with a huge troop of fighters, they rushed to pass a law limiting the number of gladiators anyone could keep in Rome! In fact, Julius became such a troublemaker, he was forced to leave the Senate in disgrace.

Impressive speaker

Julius was an impressive speaker. He persuaded many people to take his side and before long he was back in his old seat in the Senate. From then on he used his abilities to win friends and influence people. When that did not work, he bribed people to vote for his party, and got himself elected high priest! But Julius made many enemies along the way. Roman politics was a dangerous business—people changed sides all the time. No one could be trusted.

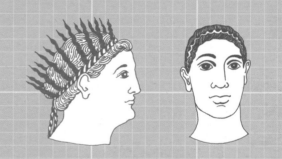

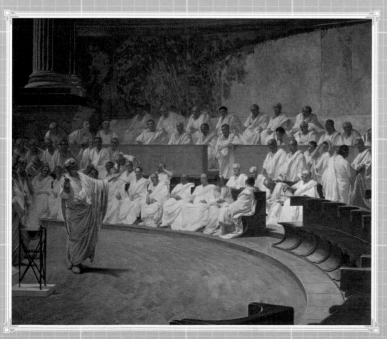

Tricky teamwork

When Julius was elected consul, the most important office in Rome, he knew he needed all the support he could get. He set up his friends, Marcus Crassus and Gnaeus Pompey, as fellow consuls. The three of them were not very honest, but they made a powerful team. Crassus had the money, Pompey had the army, and Julius had the ambition. Together they took over the Senate, swearing to oppose any law they did not like. At last Julius could push through laws that would advance his career!

"So he became powerful," said Hannah.

"Yes, he was a consul," said Colonel Karbuncle, "a member of the city council, but consuls could only rule for a few years at a time, so Julius had to do something else. Usually ex-consuls automatically became governors of outlying provinces in the Roman Empire.

Julius looked around to see which would suit him best and chose Gaul—that's Germany, Austria, and France to you and me. He hoped this move would bring him the success and wealth he wanted."

"Anyway, it was the open road for him and his armies," continued the Colonel. "And it was a fine life. According to the **memoirs** of Carbunculus, Roman soldiers had to be super fit to go on **campaign**.

"Not only did they have to march all day long, they were also weighed down by 110 pounds (50 kg) of heavy weapons and armor, not to mention a cooking pot, a spade, and pickaxe for digging trenches. Oh, and of course his sandals, just like the ones here."

"Wow! That must have been crippling!" exclaimed Digby. "Luckily, Roman roads were good and straight," Colonel Karbuncle went on, "so Julius's armies traveled in record time."

GOVERNOR OF GAUL

From 58 to 49 BC Julius Caesar **conquered** huge new territories in Gaul. He proved beyond a doubt that he was a military genius—in nine years he lost only two battles. He conquered all the territories west of the Rhine River, in what is now modern day Germany, and drove the Germanic tribes off of their lands.

Caesar's legions

Caesar had a regular army, which he made larger with **legions** raised with his own money. One legion, from Gaul, was called the Crested Lark. It was made up of 3,600 men divided into ten **cohorts**. Each cohort had six **centuries** of 60 men and was led by a **centurion**. There was also a signifier, or flag carrier, and a *cornicen*, or horn blower.

A good leader

Caesar demanded strict discipline when his armies were training. His drills had to be carried out to perfection, whether they included spear throwing, sword fighting, or just marching. No deserter went unpunished. To show he was one of them, Caesar led his men into battle, bareheaded and on foot. He stopped at nothing, and was always the first to cross a raging river or scale a mountain pass.

"What were the Gauls like?" asked Digby. "Were they what we call **barbarians**?"

"The Romans referred to anyone outside Rome as barbarians," said Colonel Karbuncle. "Could be because those tribal languages made a constant 'bababa' sound. Anyway, the barbarians in central Europe included the Celts—the ancestors of the Scottish, Irish, and Welsh. They were a fearsome bunch!"

"I guess they were pretty brave warriors, though," said Hannah.

"Goodness me, yes," agreed the Colonel. "When they got ready to do battle, they painted their bodies with swirling patterns using a blue plant dye called woad. Then they washed clay into their hair and combed it so it stood up on end. And before a fight they'd blow their war horns, sing rowdy songs, yell terrible insults at each other, and boast of their bravery—just to get themselves into a vicious mood."

"What did they wear?" asked Hannah.

"Most of them went into battle wearing little more than heavy metal anklets and bracelets which they thought of as good luck charms," said Colonel Karbuncle.

"They fought with huge battle axes, didn't they?" asked Digby.

"They did my boy. But they were also great horsemen and charioteers. In fact, they were so good that whenever the Romans captured them, they were put straight into the Roman cavalry."

BARBARIAN TRIBES

Caesar was determined to conquer the barbarian tribes. Some Gauls tried to rebel against Roman rule, but Caesar put down any revolt quickly and brutally. His victories made him popular back home in Rome. Each triumph meant more celebrations and public holidays, and increased his soldiers' devotion—although the Senate didn't always agree with his methods.

Raids on Britain

Caesar raided the island of Britain twice, in 55 and 54 BC. Legend has it that he went there because he was told he would find rare freshwater pearls along its shores. In fact, he wanted to teach the Britons a lesson for helping the Gauls fight against him.

Britons defeated

As his ships approached the south coast, fierce Britons lined up along the white cliffs, banging their shields with their battle axes. More warriors plunged into the waves to prevent Caesar's ships from reaching the beach, but they were no match for the disciplined Romans. Caesar set up camp before some of his ships were destroyed by a storm. Then he accepted the surrender of the Britons before setting sail again. His second expedition saw troops move 93 miles (150 km) inland where they faced the barbarian hordes of the warlike Cassivellaunus. But the Britons were beaten back again and agreed to pay tribute to Rome. Afterwards, Caesar quickly returned to Gaul to put down a rebellion.

ROMANS AND CELTS

Celtic tribes had been harassing northern Italy for hundreds of years. Caesar wanted to drive them away, or make them part of the Roman Empire. Unlike some of their Asian enemies, the Celts, Britons, and Teutonic tribes seemed uncivilized. This meant that they were treated with little respect, although Caesar secretly admired their fierce bravery on the battlefield. In his diaries, he remarked how they showed no fear, and drove their chariots into his legions, leapt down, and fought hand-to-hand.

Vercingetorix, a Celtic leader was captured and taken to Rome. Although he was a king, he was left in prison to die.

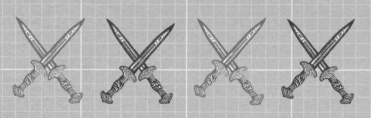

Barbarian captives

Most captive Britons and Celts were sold as slaves, although some became gladiators and served out their lives in Rome. Caesar also liked to exhibit them in his triumphs. Rebellious chieftains or leaders were often strangled during the ceremonies to display the power of Rome.

Battle banquets

One of the reasons the barbarian hordes, including the Celts, could not stand up to the Roman armies is that they lacked discipline. There were too many tribes, and too many leaders. They also liked to enjoy themselves too much, even before a battle. They would eat and drink themselves into a stupor instead of preparing like the Romans did.

Songs and stories

We do not know much about the Celts because they did not write, but communicated by word of mouth. They liked to recite long poems and sing songs—mostly about how brave they were in battle. The Romans wrote about them, and told of how they lived in tribes, worshiped nature, and had Druid priests.

Human sacrifices

Druid priests led religious ceremonies by a lakeside or within a circle made of stone or wood. The Sun, Moon, and stars were important to the Celtic people, and represented gods. The tribal ways of the barbarians were completely foreign to the Romans who persecuted the Druids. They probably did not like the idea of human sacrifice that the Celts sometimes practiced on the Beltain festival of May 1st. In fact, Caesar mentioned "wicker-men" in his diaries—referring to the Celtic practice of putting live victims inside body-shaped wicker baskets, and burning them as sacrifices to their god, Belenos.

"The Romans must have loved Caesar," said Digby. "Especially as he gave them lots of festivals and holidays."

"The ordinary people loved him," agreed Colonel Karbuncle, "but the Senate was full of discontent and back-stabbing. Pompey, Caesar's fellow consul, thought Caesar was getting far too big for his boots. And perhaps he was. Caesar's ambition had gotten out of control—and he had put together a big army, which made everyone nervous!"

"Then the Senate decided they only wanted one consul in the future, and that was to be Pompey," said Mr. Rummage.

"So what did Julius do?" asked Hannah. "He did what he always did—he bribed and threatened people to get what he wanted," said Mr. Rummage.

"The only problem was," added the Colonel, "he was still in Gaul! A senator proposed that Caesar's army should be disbanded, and that Caesar shouldn't be allowed back as consul," said the Colonel.

"Caesar was furious. He believed he was 'the leading Roman of the day.' He took his armies across the Alps and camped near the side of the Rubicon River, which formed the frontier between Gaul and Roman Italy. Civil war looked likely, and he told his men that once across the river, there was no way back. They would have to fight on."

"Was there a huge battle?" asked Digby.

"There were lots of battles all over the place—in Italy, Spain, and Greece—but the armies of the Senate couldn't defeat Caesar," said the Colonel.

THE RUBICON

Standing on the northern bank of the Rubicon River, Julius Caesar faced the most difficult decision of his life. He knew that if he crossed the Rubicon, he would be committing an act of treason. He also knew that if he returned to Rome without his army, he would be defenseless against his enemies. He feared he would be brought to trial for the dishonest way he handled his first consulship. He believed the Senate would condemn him to death regardless of his victories in Gaul.

Caesar's vision

While Caesar was wondering what to do next, legend has it that a ghost of superhuman size appeared by the river playing a reed pipe. Soldiers gathered round to listen to the music. Then the ghost snatched a trumpet from one of the soldiers and gave a long loud blast. Caesar saw this as a message to cross the river. "Let us accept this as a sign from the gods, and follow where they beckon... The die is cast." It was the start of civil war.

Friends and foes

When Caesar's old friend and fellow consul, Crassus, was killed in battle, Pompey became his number one enemy. Caesar made short work of Pompey's army in Greece in 48 BC. Pompey then fled to Egypt, where he tried to raise another army. Caesar knew that, sooner or later, he would have to deal with him again.

"So when did it all end—the Roman civil war, I mean?" asked Hannah.

"It went on for ages," said Colonel Karbuncle. "So long, in fact, that Caesar was in danger of running out of money to fund his armies. He needed more money, so he decided to go to Egypt."

"Was he chasing Pompey?" asked Digby.

"No, no," replied the Colonel, "apparently the **pharaoh** of Egypt owed Caesar a hefty sum. So Caesar went there to collect it."

"Knowing him, he got what he wanted," said Hannah smiling.

"He got more than he bargained for," said the Colonel. "He got the queen herself. Yes, he met the beautiful and very smart Cleopatra—and was instantly taken with her."

"The story goes," said Mr. Rummage, "that when Caesar entered the capital city of Alexandria, he seized the palace and ordered Cleopatra and her brother Ptolemy to meet him. They were squabbling over who should rule Egypt. Cleopatra was determined to have the throne to herself, so she had herself smuggled into Caesar's heavily guarded rooms wrapped in a bedroll. Luckily for her, Caesar decided to back her claim to the throne instead of her brother's."

"She was a smart woman," said the Colonel.

"What happened to her brother?" asked Digby, changing the subject.

"Caesar's armies defeated him in battle," replied the Colonel. "The next day, his body was found floating in the harbor."

POWER AT LAST!

The "empire"

A brilliant politician and general, Caesar had achieved a lot for the glory of Rome and her people. Because of his strength as a military leader, many different lands had been added to Rome's territory, including Spain and France to the west, the German lands west of the Alps, and Italy, Greece, and Asia Minor to the East. Much of North Africa, including Egypt, would also become part of the empire.

Caesar's changes

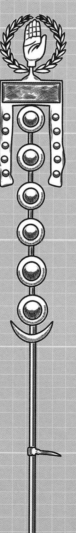

While he was in power, Caesar made many important changes. He opened the Senate to men who were not nobles. He also launched massive building projects, passed new laws, and changed the outdated tax and voting systems. His new laws made him very popular with ordinary people, but very unpopular with the nobles in the Senate.

Dictator for life

Among the main changes the Senate did not like was Caesar's decision to make himself dictator-for-life. From now on, no one could oppose him on penalty of death. This was against Roman law, but Caesar did not stop there. He had a statue of himself erected among the ancient kings of Rome, and he had a golden throne put in the Senate house, and another in the tribunal. He also renamed the seventh month of the year, July, in honor of himself!

"**I** guess all the power was going to his head," suggested Digby. "I mean, if I had all that power, I suppose I'd want to do everything my way. I'd make Hannah governor of Outer Mongolia for a start."

"Then you might also end up like Caesar," hinted Mr. Rummage. "And you certainly wouldn't want that."

"Not a bit," laughed Colonel Karbuncle. "Of course, Caesar should have listened to his wife a bit more."

"What do you mean?" asked Hannah.

"Well Calpurnia had a dream," said Mr. Rummage mysteriously. "She dreamed that her husband, the mighty Caesar, would be struck down and die a violent death."

"It sounds more like a nightmare," said Digby.

"Well, Calpurnia was a bit nervous at the best of times," said the Colonel.

"But was she right?" asked Hannah.

"She was," said the Colonel. "The senators and tribunes and powerful Romans were against Caesar now. The only way they thought they could get rid of him was to assassinate him."

"You mean kill him?" asked Digby in astonishment.

"Yes," said the Colonel. "The only question was how and where."

"So when they learned that Caesar had called a meeting at the Assembly Rooms for the 15th of March—known as the Ides of March—they decided to do it then."

"Then there were the **omens**," said Colonel Karbuncle. "The horses Caesar had dedicated to the Rubicon River began to shed tears, and a wise man told him that danger would continue to threaten him until the Ides of March."

"But Caesar ignored the omens and went to the Assembly Rooms where the senators awaited him," said Mr. Rummage. "Then they struck—twenty-three dagger thrusts. And Rome's greatest soldier was no more."

"Phew!" said Digby. "I wouldn't want to be in his shoes. But all the same, I'll take the sandals, Mr. Rummage."

ASSASSINATED!

The senators had murdered Caesar in order to stop him from becoming king. They were trying to save the republic. But their actions only plunged Rome back into the grip of civil war. And the next Caesar, Julius's grandnephew Gaius Octavius, would become the first emperor, and establish the empire they had tried so hard to prevent.

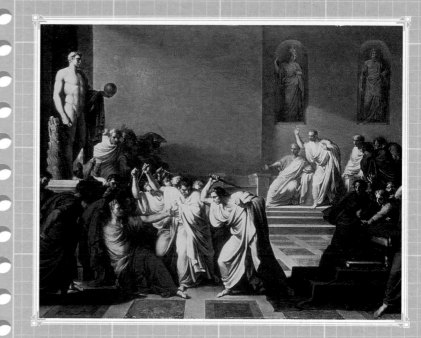

Caesar the god

After Julius Caesar's death, the senators who were loyal to him pronounced that he should be deified, or be worshiped as a god. This seemed the right move to make since, on the day of his funeral games, a comet appeared in the sky and stayed there for seven days!

Gaius Julius Caesar was murdered to prevent republican Rome from becoming a monarchy again. But it happened anyway, except that the men who followed in his footsteps were honored as emperors, not just kings, and some were even worshiped as gods. In his will, Caesar left his grandnephew and adopted son, Gaius Octavius, three quarters of his estate. Octavius adopted the name Augustus and became the first proper emperor in 2 BC.

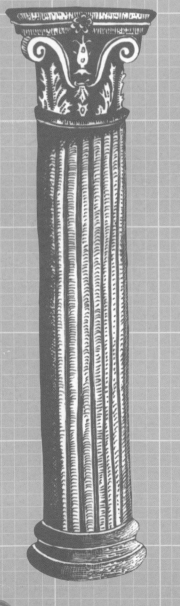

Julius Caesar is remembered not just as a military genius, but as a great speaker and politician. Under his leadership he made much of Western Europe a province of Rome. During his military campaigns, he experienced only a handful of setbacks. He dominated the Senate when he was in Rome, both with his powerful presence and his witty and persuasive speeches to the public. His death marked the beginning of the change in Rome from a republic to an empire. The empire would survive for another 500 years.

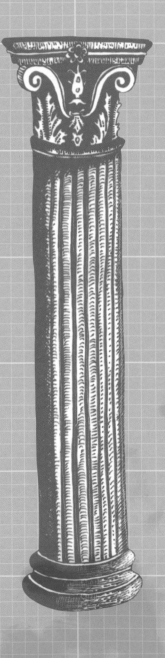

Glossary

arcade A covered walkway

barbarians A person living outside of the empire

campaign An organized military operation

century A Roman army of 60-100 soldiers

centurion The leader of a Roman army of 100 men

cohort A Roman army of 600 men

conquer To overcome and control with military force

consul One of two men elected for the highest position in the Roman Empire. Consuls were responsible for war, justice, and finance

empire A large group of states or countries, under the leadership of one ruling authority

legion An army of 3,000 to 6,000 Roman soldiers

magistrate A political officer elected by citizens

memoirs A record of the personal experiences of the author

omen An event or object that is seen as having a connection to foretell the future

pharaoh An ancient ruler of Egypt

republic A society ruled by officers elected by its citizens

sesterces A form of ancient Roman money

talent A unit of money used in ancient Rome

Index

Alexander the Great 11, 20

assassination 34, 35, 36

Britons 25, 26

Calpurnia 31, 34

Celts 24, 26, 27

civil war 28, 29, 30, 35

Cleopatra 30, 31

Cornelia 13

Egypt 29, 30, 31, 33

festivals 20, 27, 28, 32

Forum 18, 20

Gaius Octavius 35, 36

Gauls 22, 23, 24, 25, 28, 29

gladiators 14, 15, 16, 17, 21, 26

gods 11, 15, 20, 27, 29, 32, 35, 36

Pompey 21, 28, 29, 30, 31, 32

republic 9, 20, 21, 32, 35, 36

Roman Empire 9, 18, 22, 26, 33, 36

Rubicon River 28, 29, 35

Senate 21, 25, 28, 29, 32, 33, 36

Other characters in the Stories of Great People series.

SAFFRON sells pots and pans, herbs, spices, oils, soaps, and dyes from her spice kitchen stall.

BUZZ is a street vendor with all the gossip. He sells candies from a tray that's strapped around his neck.

PRU is a dreamer and Hannah's best friend. She likes to visit the market with Digby and Hannah, especially when makeup and dressing up is involved.

PIXIE the market's fortuneteller sells incense, lotions, and potions, candles, mandalas, and crystals inside her exotic stall.

JAKE is Digby's friend. He's got a lively imagination and is always up to mischief.

Mr. POLLOCK's toy stall is filled with string puppets, rocking horses, model planes, wooden animals—and he makes them all himself!

Printed in the U.S.A. – CG